The Art of Jewish Living
The Passover Seder

A Workbook

by
Dr. Ron Wolfson
with **Joel Lurie Grishaver**

A project of The Federation of Jewish Men's Clubs
and
The University of Judaism

The Federation of Jewish Men's Clubs, an arm of the Conservative Movement, trains lay leadership and promotes Jewish education in the home and synagogue.

The University of Judaism is an academic institution dedicated to the study and enhancement of Jewish life.

Alef Type and Design provided all typesetting and design services for *The Art of Jewish Living* series.

ISBN #0935665-20-X
Illustrations © Lisa Rauchwerger

© 1988 Federation of Jewish Men's Clubs
475 Riverside Drive, Suite 244
New York, NY 10015

Published by Jewish Lights Publishing
www.jewishlights.com
ISBN: 978-1-879045-94-1 (pbk.)

Welcome to Passover University

INTRODUCTION

The Art of Jewish Living series, a project of the Federation of Jewish Men's Clubs and the University of Judaism, is a program designed to enable adult learners to master the skills required for meaningful Jewish observance. *The Art of Jewish Living: The Passover Seder* is a course of study designed to teach the meanings and competencies for creating a Passover and Seder experience in the home.

This book is the Student Workbook for *The Art of Jewish Living: The Passover Seder* course. It is the companion volume to *The Art of Jewish Living: The Passover Seder* Student Textbook, written by Dr. Ron Wolfson, with Joel Lurie Grishaver. Together with an available Audiocassette featuring the chants of the Passover Seder, these materials represent the core curriculum of the *AJL: Passover Seder* course.

We have envisioned this program as a "mini-Passover University", complete with a sequence of courses and electives designed to impart a specific set of skills and a body of information to you, the learner. These courses are:

PESAH 101: UNDERSTANDING THE SEDER

a three-session course on Seder leading, including an overview of the Seder's structure, a demonstration of the Seder ceremony, and instructions on editing the *Haggadah* and tips on great Seder leading.

PESAH 201: PREPARING FOR *PESAH*

a three-session course on preparing the home for Passover, consisting of instructions on *kashering* ("making fit") the kitchen, *Pesah* shopping, and conducting the rituals of Passover preparation.

PESAH 301: *HAGGADAH* FLUENCY

a three-session course providing instruction and practice in reading and chanting the original texts of the *Haggadah*.

PESAH 401: *PESAH* SEDER LEADING

a three-session course on how to study the *midrashic* sections of the *Haggadah*, how to make personal *midrash*, and creative ideas for Seder leading.

PESAH 501: INVOLVING CHILDREN IN THE PASSOVER EXPERIENCE

a one-session elective offering strategies for involving young children in the Seder experience.

PESAH 601: CREATIVE PASSOVER COOKERY

a one-session elective for sharing *Pesah* recipes, menus, and creative ideas for table presentation.

You have probably enrolled in one of the above courses and received a copy of this Workbook, as well as a copy of the Student Textbook and Audiocassette. The Workbook contains a number of worksheets that you will complete as the course unfolds. Your instructor will guide you to the appropriate section for the course you have chosen. By completing the exercises and taking notes on the information presented in each course, you will accumulate a body of knowledge which will be a valuable resource for your Passover celebrations for years to come.

We wish you *"b'hatzlahah,"* good success on learning *The Art of Jewish Living!*

Table of Contents

PESAH 101: UNDERSTANDING THE SEDER

Objectives:

1. To recall memories of Seder experiences.
2. To discuss what makes a great Seder leader
3. To learn the structure of the Seder ceremony.
4. To learn how to set the Seder table.
5. To learn the meanings of the symbolic foods of the Seder.
6. To begin the process of editing your *Haggadah*.

SEDER MEMORIES

A *Pesah* Seder is as much a folk creation as it is a formal ritual procedure. Each family and each community creates its own expression of how to celebrate the Exodus from Egypt. Our own memories of Seder, and the Seder patterns we have experienced, are very much part of the way we create our own Seder rituals. Therefore, we begin our learning about how to create our own dynamic Seder with remembering what we already know from our own Seder experiences.

Fill in your own Seder memories.

My earliest memory of Seder is_____

_____

_____

The best thing at Seder was_____

_____

_____

The worst thing at Seder was_____

_____

_____

My favorite part of the Seder was_____

_____

_____

The guests at the Seder included _____

_____

_____

The leader of the Seder was_____

_____

_____

The funniest thing that ever happened at a Seder was_____

_____

_____

One night, when we opened the door for Elijah,_____

_____

_____

The best *afikomen* hiding place was_____

_____

_____

The best *afikomen* present was_____

_____

_____

The best Seder I ever attended was_____

_____

_____

because_____

_____

_____

WHAT MAKES A GREAT SEDER LEADER?

Through the time spent in the Passover University you can become a master Seder leader. By completing the sessions you are attending, you will both know more about the Seder and how it works and expand your skills at being a great leader. Use this page to set the target for this growth. Make a list of behaviors which a great Seder leader manifests. These are skills you are going to acquire.

Great Seder leaders _____

_____

_____

_____

_____

_____

_____

_____

_____

_____

_____

_____

_____

_____

_____

_____

_____

_____

_____

_____

_____

_____

_____

_____

_____

_____

_____

_____

_____

_____

Pesah 101
Activity Three: The Structure of the Seder
Purpose: *To learn the structure of the Seder experience.*

THE STRUCTURE OF THE SEDER

Your instructor is going to introduce you to the structure and order of the Passover Seder. Use the following pages to take your notes. When you are done, you'll understand that the Seder is really a very simple and logical progression of steps.

ACT ONE—THE BEGINNING

PROLOGUE

_____

_____

_____

_____

SCENE 1: *KADESH* (THE FIRST CUP)

_____

_____

_____

_____

SCENE 2: *URHATZ* (WASH HANDS)

_____

_____

_____

_____

SCENE 3: *KARPAS* (APPETIZER)

_____

_____

_____

_____

SCENE 4: *YAHATZ* (BREAK THE MIDDLE *MATZAH*)

_____

_____

_____

_____

CURTAIN: *HA LAHMA ANYA* (INVITATION)

ACT TWO—*MAGGID* (THE TELLINGS)

SCENE 1: THE FIRST TELLING

_____
_____
_____
_____

SCENE 2: THE SECOND TELLING

_____
_____
_____
_____

SCENE 3: THE THIRD TELLING

_____
_____
_____
_____

SCENE 4: THE FOURTH TELLING

_____
_____
_____
_____

CURTAIN: *KOS SHEINI* (THE SECOND CUP)

_____
_____
_____
_____

ACT THREE—THE FEAST

SCENE 1: PREPARING TO EAT

_____
_____
_____
_____
_____
_____

SCENE 2: *SHULḤAN OREKH* (SET THE TABLE)

_____
_____
_____
_____

SCENE 3: *TZAFUN* (*AFIKOMEN*)

_____
_____
_____
_____
_____

SCENE 4: *BAREKH* (BLESSINGS AFTER FOOD)

_____
_____
_____
_____

CURTAIN: *KOS SH'LISHI* (THE THIRD CUP)

_____
_____
_____
_____

ACT FOUR—REDEMPTION

SCENE 1: *SHFOKH ḤAMATKHA* ("POUR OUT YOUR WRATH")
            ELIYAHU HA-NAVI (ELIJAH THE PROPHET)

_____

_____

_____

_____

SCENE 2: *HALLEL* (SONGS OF PRAISE)

_____

_____

_____

_____

SCENE 3: *Z'MIROT* (SONGS)

_____

_____

_____

_____

SCENE 4: *SEFIRAT HA-OMER* (COUNTING OF THE OMER)

_____

_____

_____

_____

CURTAIN: *KOS R'VI'I* (THE FOURTH CUP)
            NIRTZAH (ACCEPTANCE)

_____

_____

_____

_____

THE TALK FEAST IN FOUR ACTS

The Seder is a talk-feast in four acts. The *Haggadah* is the script for the evening. Below you will find an outline of the *Haggadah*. Since there are very different editions of the *Haggadah* in use, it is important to locate where each step of the Seder is found in your text.

Take your *Haggadah* in hand and flip through it to find each step. As you do, fill the "page" number in the outline.

(When you are reading to assign parts for the Seder, complete the "Who" column. Hint: Use pencil--the assignments are likely to change from year-to-year.)

Step	Page	Items	Practice	Who

ACT ONE: THE BEGINNING

Prologue

Step	Page	Items	Practice	Who
Candle Lighting	____	Candles Candlesticks Matches	Light Candles	_____
Kadesh, Urhatz	____	Text	Say or chant	_____

SCENE 1: THE FIRST CUP

Kadesh	____	First cup	Lift cup of wine, chant and drink while reclining together.	_____

SCENE 2: HANDS

Urhatz	____	Water Pitcher Basin Towel	Wash without blessing	_____

SCENE 3: APPETIZER

Karpas	____	Vegetable (parsley) Salt water	Dip parsley in salt water, recite blessing together.	_____

SCENE 4: BREAK THE MIDDLE *MATZAH*

Yahatz	____	Middle *Matzah*	Leader breaks *matzah* in two; hides *afikomen*.	_____

CURTAIN: INVITATION

Ha Lahma Anya	____	*Matzot*	Uncover *matzot*, recite.	_____

14

Step	Page	Items	Practice	Who

ACT TWO: *MAGGID*—THE TELLINGS

SCENE 1: THE FIRST TELLING

Step	Page	Items	Practice	Who
Question: *Mah Nishtanah*	_____	Wine cup *Matzot*	Cover *matzot*; fill 2nd cup; recite	_____
Answer: *Avadim Hayinu*	_____	*Matzot*	Uncover *matzot*; recite	_____
Praise: *Barukh Ha-Makom*	_____	Text	Recite together	_____

SCENE 2: THE SECOND TELLING

Step	Page	Items	Practice	Who
Question: *Arba'ah Banim*	_____	Text 4 children	Recite	_____
Answer: *Miteḥila Ovdei*	_____	Text	Recite	_____
Praise: *Barukh Shomer/* *V'hi She'amdah*	_____ _____	Wine cup	Raise cup; sing together	_____

SCENE 3: THE THIRD TELLING

Step	Page	Items	Practice	Who
Question: *Tzei u-L'mad*	_____	Text	Uncover *matzot*; recite	_____
Answer: *Arami oved avi* *Eser Makot*	_____ _____	Text Wine cup	Recite Spill one drop for each plague	_____ _____
Praise: *Dayyenu*	_____	Text	Sing together	_____

SCENE 4: THE FOURTH TELLING

Step	Page	Items	Practice	Who
Question: *Rabban Gamliel*	_____	Text	Recite; point to symbols	_____
Answer: *B'khol dor va-Dor*	_____	Text	Recite	_____
Praise: *L'fikhakh*	_____	Wine cup	Lift and recite	_____
V'nomar L'fanav *Ga'al Yisrael*	_____ _____	Text Wine cup	Recite Lift and recite	_____ _____

CURTAIN: THE SECOND CUP OF WINE

Step	Page	Items	Practice	Who
Kos Sheini	_____	Wine cup	Lift and chant; drink while reclining	_____

ACT THREE: THE FEAST

SCENE 1: PREPARING TO EAT

Step	Page	Items	Practice	Who
Roḥtzah	⎯⎯	Water Pitcher, basin, towel	All wash hands; recite	⎯⎯⎯
Motzi/Matzah	⎯⎯	*Matzot*	Lift three *matzot* Recite both blessings; eat piece of top and/or middle *matzah* while reclining	⎯⎯⎯
Maror	⎯⎯	*Maror*, Ḥaroset	Dip *maror* in Ḥaroset recite blessing; eat without reclining	⎯⎯⎯
Korekh	⎯⎯	Bottom *matzah*, *maror*	Make sandwich of *maror* between two pieces of *matzah*, recite and eat without reclining.	⎯⎯⎯

SCENE 2: THE MEAL

Step	Page	Items	Practice	Who
Shulḥan Orekh	⎯⎯	Food	Enjoy!	

SCENE 3: THE *AFIKOMEN*

Step	Page	Items	Practice	Who
Tzafun	⎯⎯	*Afikomen*	*Afikomen* is redeemed; eat a piece while reclining.	⎯⎯⎯

SCENE 4: BLESSINGS AFTER FOOD

Step	Page	Items	Practice	Who
Barekh	⎯⎯	Wine	Fill third cup; recite *Birkat ha-Mazon*	⎯⎯⎯

CURTAIN: THE THIRD CUP OF WINE

Step	Page	Items	Practice	Who
Kos Sh'lishi	⎯⎯	Wine	Lift, recite drink while reclining	⎯⎯⎯

Step	Page	Items	Practice	Who

ACT FOUR: REDEMPTION

SCENE 1: ELIJAH THE PROPHET

Step	Page	Items	Practice	Who
Shfokh Ḥamatkha	____	Text	Fill Elijah's wine Cup and Fourth Cup; open door; recite	_____
Eliyahu ha-Navi	____	Text; Elijah's cup	Sing together; Elijah's cup is not moved	_____

SCENE 2: SONGS OF PRAISE

Step	Page	Items	Practice	Who
Hallel	____	Text	Sing, recite	_____

SCENE 3: SONGS

Step	Page	Items	Practice	Who
Z'mirot	____	Text	Sing together	_____

SCENE 4: COUNTING THE OMER (SECOND SEDER ONLY)

Step	Page	Items	Practice	Who
Sefirat ha-Omer	____	Text	Rise and recite	_____

CURTAIN: CONCLUSION

Step	Page	Items	Practice	Who
Kos R'vi'i (Fourth Cup)	____	Wine	Lift cup; recite; drink while reclining	_____
Nirtzah	____	Text	Recite together	_____

SEDER PREPARATION CHECKLIST

_____ 1. CANDLESTICKS

_____ 2. CANDLES

_____ 3. *KIPPOT*

_____ 4. WHITE TABLECLOTH

_____ 5. PLACE SETTING

_____ 6. FLOWERS

_____ 7. PLACECARDS

_____ 8. SEDER CARDS

_____ 9. WINE CUP

_____ 10. CUP OF ELIJAH

_____ 11. WINE

_____ 12. *MATZAH*

_____ 13. *MATZAH COVER*

_____ 14. *AFIKOMEN* HOLDER

_____ 15. SALT WATER

_____ 16. *HAGGADOT*

_____ 17. WATER PITCHER, BASIN AND TOWEL

_____ 18. HARD-BOILED EGGS

_____ 19. PILLOWS

_____ 20. SEDER PLATE

Activity Six: The Items on the Seder Plate
Purpose: *To learn the name and location of each object.*

SCHEMATIC OF THE SEDER PLATE

Here is a diagram of the Seder plate. Translate each of the Hebrew names below:

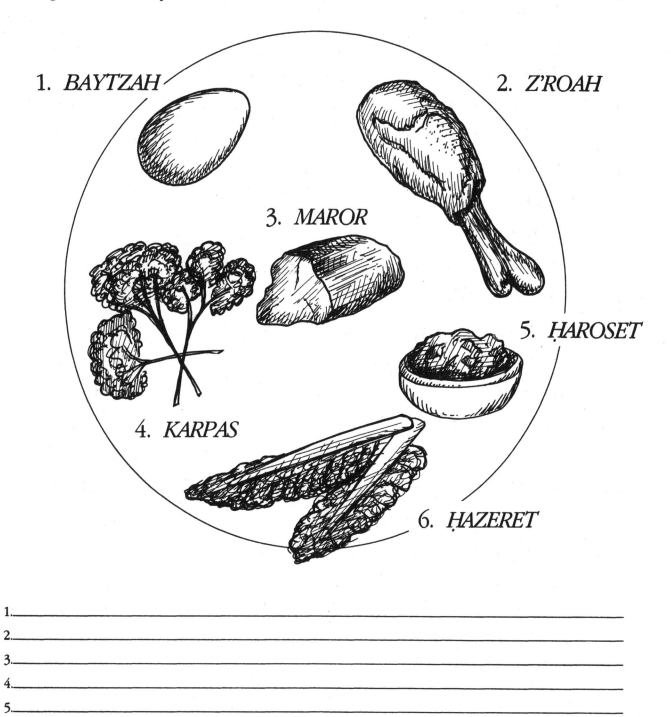

1. *BAYTZAH*

2. *Z'ROAH*

3. *MAROR*

5. *ḤAROSET*

4. *KARPAS*

6. *ḤAZERET*

1._____

2._____

3._____

4._____

5._____

6._____

Pesah 101
Activity Seven: The Objects on the Seder Plate
Purpose: *To learn the symbolic explanation of each object.*

THE SEDER PLATE

In the place provided, identify the explanation of each of the six symbolic foods on the Seder plate:

_____ *Z'ROAH* (SHANKBONE)

The reasons:_____

_____

_____ *BAYTZAH* (ROASTED EGG)

The reasons:_____

_____

_____ *MAROR* (BITTER HERBS)

The reasons:_____

_____

_____ *HAROSET* (MIXTURE)

The reasons:_____

_____

_____ *KARPAS* (GREENS)

The reasons:_____

_____

_____ *HAZERET* (SECOND BITTER HERB)

The reasons:_____

_____

MATZAH

There are three ceremonial *matzot* placed near the Seder plate. Identify their use:

TOP *MATZAH*   USED FOR_____

MIDDLE *MATZAH*   USED FOR_____

BOTTOM *MATZAH*   USED FOR_____

Some use a fourth *matzah*, the *Matzah* of Hope. What does this symbolize when it is used in the Seder?

_____

_____

EXPLANATIONS

There are a number of different explanations of the symbolism of the three *matzot*. My favorite explanation is that the *matzot* stand for:

_____

The top *matzah* stands for:_____

The middle *matzah* stands for:_____

The bottom *matzah* stands for:_____

THE DEMONSTRATION SEDER

I n class, you are going to work your way through a demonstration Seder. As you watch and participate, use these pages to take notes and to record your questions.

NOTES

_____

_____

_____

_____

_____

_____

_____

_____

_____

_____

_____

_____

_____

_____

_____

_____

_____

_____

_____

_____

_____

_____

_____

_____

_____

_____

_____

_____

_____

NOTES

EDITING YOUR *HAGGADAH*

N ow that you have learned the basic structure of the Seder ceremony, it is time to make some decisions about the content of your Seder experience. To do this, you must first edit your *Haggadah*.

Here is a list of the major sections of the *Haggadah*.

First, use the following code to guess what Jewish law says about each step. Fill in the first column of boxes.

> N = Necessary
> D = Desirable
> A = Additional

In the second column, record the answers given by your instructor. In the third column, make your own choices about what steps of the *Haggadah* you consider: Necessary, Desirable, or Additional.

ACT ONE: The Beginning

Prologue: Candle Lighting	——	——	——
Kadesh, Urhatz Mnemonic	——	——	——
Kadesh (Kiddush)	——	——	——
Urhatz	——	——	——
Karpas	——	——	——
Yahatz	——	——	——
Ha Lahma Anya	——	——	——

ACT TWO: *Maggid*–The Tellings

Mah Nishtanah	——	——	——
Avadim Hayinu	——	——	——
Barukh ha-Makom	——	——	——
Arba'ah Banim	——	——	——
Metihila Ovdei Avodah Zarah	——	——	——
Barukh Shomer/V'hi She'amdah	——	——	——
Tzei u'L-mad	——	——	——
Arami Oved Avi	——	——	——
Eser Makot	——	——	——
Dayyenu	——	——	——
Rabban Gamliel Hayah Omer	——	——	——

B'khol Dor va-Dor	____	____	____
L'fikhakh	____	____	____
V'nomar L'fanav	____	____	____
Ga'al Yisrael	____	____	____
Kos Sheini	____	____	____

ACT THREE: The Feast

Rohtzah	____	____	____
Motzi/Matzah	____	____	____
Maror	____	____	____
Korekh	____	____	____
Shulhan Orekh	____	____	____
Tzafun	____	____	____
Barekh	____	____	____
Kos Sh'lishi	____	____	____

ACT FOUR: Redemption

Shfokh Hamatkha	____	____	____
Eliyahu ha-Navi	____	____	____
Hallel	____	____	____
Z'mirot	____	____	____
Sefirat ha-Omer	____	____	____
Kos R'vi'i	____	____	____
Nirtzah	____	____	____
Matzah of Hope	____	____	____
Kos Hamishi (The Fifth Cup)	____	____	____

My Choices for Seder

My favorite step of the Seder is_____

My least favorite step of the Seder is_____

The easiest step of the Seder is_____

The most difficult step of the Seder is_____

Seder steps I shouldn't leave out_____

_____

_____

WHAT I KNOW/WHAT I NEED WORK ON

Here are two lists. In the first list, write down the parts of the Seder you feel comfortable doing now. In the second, write down the parts of the Seder you need to learn more about.

WHAT I KNOW   **WHAT I NEED WORK ON**

_____   _____

_____   _____

_____   _____

_____   _____

_____   _____

_____   _____

_____   _____

_____   _____

_____   _____

_____   _____

PESAH 201: PREPARING FOR *PESAH*

Objectives:

1. To identify foods that must be removed from one's possession during Passover.
2. To learn which foods require rabbinic certification and when to be considered acceptable for Passover.
3. To learn how to *kasher* utensils for *Pesah*.
4. To review the steps of conducting a *Bedikat Hametz* ritual.

KOSHER FOR *PESAH*—
WHAT TO REMOVE

The first job in preparing the home to be kosher for Passover is to remove any and all traces of *hametz*. *Hametz* is defined as food containing any amount of leavened product derived from five types of grain: wheat, barley, oats, spelt and rye. Here is a list of some of the most common forms of *hametz*:

_____ Leavened bread
_____ Rolls
_____ Bagels
_____ Muffins
_____ Biscuits
_____ Croissants
_____ Doughnuts
_____ Crackers
_____ Cakes
_____ Cereals
_____ Coffee with cereal additives
_____ Wheat
_____ Spelt
_____ Rye
_____ Oats
_____ Barley
_____ Liquor made with grain alcohol (e.g. scotch, bourbon, gin, etc.)
_____ Any opened can or jar of processed food
_____ Any opened container of dairy product, margarine, butter or cheese

Kitniot (for *Ashkenazim*):

_____ Rice
_____ Corn
_____ Millet
_____ Legumes (beans and peas)
_____ Mustard

PESAḤ SHOPPING LIST

T he key to easy Passover shopping is knowing what foods are considered acceptable for *Pesaḥ* use with or without certification by rabbinic authority.

Here is a list of foods. Place each food in the correct category. (Beware: some foods may be listed in more than one category.)

_____ Fresh fruit

_____ Green beans

_____ Eggs

_____ Butter

_____ Margarine

_____ Cottage cheese

_____ Canned goods

_____ Fresh Fish

_____ Potato chips

_____ Ketchup

_____ Noodles

_____ Peanuts

_____ Soda

_____ Tea

_____ Yogurt

_____ Fresh meat

_____ Coffee

_____ Baking Soda

_____ Frozen uncooked fruit

_____ Ice cream

_____ Tuna in water

_____ Chocolate milk

_____ Processed foods

_____ Pickles

_____ Candy

_____ Ripened cheeses

_____ Cream cheese

_____ Liquor

_____ Spices

_____ Vinegar

_____ Pure fruit juices

_____ Fresh vegetables

_____ Wine

_____ Honey

_____ Pepper

_____ Salt

_____ Sugar

_____ Grape juice

_____ Mayonnaise

_____ Processed cheese (American / Velveeta)

A. Foods which DO NOT REQUIRE rabbinic certification AT ANY TIME

B. Foods which DO NOT REQUIRE rabbinic certification if purchased BEFORE *Pesaḥ*

C. Foods which REQUIRE rabbinic certification AT ALL TIMES

D. Foods which REQUIRE rabbinic certification if purchased DURING *Pesaḥ*

PASSOVER SHOPPING GUIDE

Foods which do not require rabbinic certification at any time:

Eggs
Fresh fruit
Fresh meat and poultry
Fresh vegetables (except *kitniot*)
Oils (Linseed and cottonseed)
Peanuts

Explanation:

_____

_____

_____

Foods which do not require rabbinic certification if purchased before *Pesaḥ* in unopened packages or containers:

Baking soda
Butter
Cheeses—ripened (cheddar, Muenster, Camembert)
Coffee
Cottage cheese
Cream cheese
Frozen uncooked vegetables
Frozen uncooked fruit
Fruit juices
Honey
Milk
Oils (vegetable)
Peanut Butter
Pepper
Salt
Spices
Tea
Tuna in water
Yogurt (plain)

Explanation:

_____

_____

_____

Foods that require rabbinic certification at all times:

American cheese
Baked goods (*matzah, matzah* flour, *matzah* farfel)
Candy
Canned goods
Chocolate flavored milk
Condiments (ketchup, mayonnaise)
Dried fruits
Egg noodles
Grape juice
Ice cream
Jellies
Liquor
Margarine*
Oils (corn)*
Pickles
Potato chips
Sodas
Vinegar
Wine
Yogurt (flavored)

Explanation:

_____

_____

_____

Foods that require rabbinic certification when purchased during *Pesah*:

Everything except fresh fruit and vegetables, eggs, and peanuts, including all dairy products.

Explanation:

_____

_____

_____

*Those who use oils of *kitniot* should purchase margarine made from those oils before Passover without certification.

KOSHER FOR *PESAH*—WHAT TO *KASHER*

T he laws of how to *kasher* utensils for Pesah are somewhat complex. *Kashering* a kitchen takes some planning. As you study this material in class, write your own generalized rules of what kinds of utensils can (and cannot) be *kashered* by each procedure.

HAGALAH: Immersion in boiling water

_____

_____

_____

_____

LIBUN: Fire

_____

_____

_____

_____

IRUI: Pouring boiling water over a surface

_____

_____

_____

_____

MILUI V'IRUI: Soaking in cold water

_____

_____

_____

_____

May not be *kashered* for *Pesah*

_____

_____

_____

_____

PESAḤ — KASHERING CHECKLIST

H ere is a list of common kitchen utensils that, if used during the year, must be *kashered* in order to use for Passover. On the line next to each object, place the appropriate code according to the key on the bottom of this page.

——— Pots

——— Pans

——— Microwave oven

——— Food processor

——— Sinks

——— Counter tops

——— Flatware

——— Glasses

——— China

——— Pyrex dishes

——— Toaster

——— Knives

——— Stove tops (electric)

——— Stove tops (gas)

——— Barbecue grills

——— Convection oven

——— Dishwasher

——— Table tops

——— Cupboards

——— Porcelain sink

H—*HAGALAH*: Immersion in boiling water
L—*LIBUN*: Fire
I—*IRUI*: Pouring boiling water over a surface
M—*MILUI V'IRUI*: Soaking in cold water
X—Cannot be *kashered* for Passover.

BEDIKAT ḤAMETZ/BITTUL ḤAMETZ

The rabbis worked out a unique "search and destroy" process to ritually clean a house before *Pesaḥ*. *Bedikat Hametz* is literally a search for the last few pieces of *hametz* which, when found and removed, will complete the changeover of the home. *Bittul Hametz* is the recitation of an ancient formula which nullifies any *hametz* that may have been overlooked during the search.

Here are the steps in conducting a *Bedikat Hametz* search for leaven. Number each step in the correct order of the ritual:

_____ Recite the *"Bedikat Ḥametz"* blessing, *"Al bi'ur Ḥametz."*

_____ Be sure you collect all the pieces of *hametz* that were hidden.

_____ On the night before *Pesaḥ*, immediately after sundown, someone hides ten pieces of *hametz* around the house. The "searchers" should not see where the pieces are hidden.

_____ Conduct the search, using the candle to illuminate areas. When a piece of *hametz* is found, sweep it onto the wooden spoon using the feather, and then deposit it into a container or on a paper plate.

_____ Secure all the *hametz* in the container or in a small area of the kitchen where *hametz* for the morning of *Erev Pesaḥ* is kept.

_____ After the search is concluded, recite the *Bittul Ḥametz* nullification formula, *"Kol Ḥamira."*

_____ A candle is lit.

MEKHIRAT ḤAMETZ

Another part of the rituals of preparation for *Pesah* is the "selling" of food that is not kosher for Passover which has not been destroyed. This ritual is called *Mekhirat Hametz*. It allows Jews to sell food that is not permitted during the holiday to a non-Jew. The ritual contract calls for its return at the end of the holiday.

These are the steps involved in selling your *hametz*. Number them in the correct order.

_____ Transfer ownership of your *hametz* to your agent via a "*shtar harsha'ah*," an authorization symbolized by the pulling of a handkerchief.

_____ The *hametz* is resold to the agent and ownership of the hametz reverts to you.

_____ Make a *Tzedakah* donation in honor of the person acting as agent for the sale.

_____ Store, secure, and label the *hametz* in your home.

_____ The agent sells the *hametz* to a non-Jew who owns it until the end of the holiday.

_____ Appoint your rabbi or shammes as agent for you to negotiate the sale of your *hametz*.

_____ Sign a document authorizing the agent to act on your behalf.

BI'UR ḤAMETZ

Bi'ur Ḥametz is the final ritual step in the preparation of the house. The final pieces of *hametz* have been searched for and found. Now these last pieces are burned, and a ritual formula is recited, nullifying any crumbs that have not been removed.

The steps involved in *Bi'ur Hametz*, the burning of *hametz*, are listed below. Place them in their correct order by numbering the steps.

_____ Have the pyromaniacs in your family ignite the *hametz*.

_____ Watch the *hametz* burn until it is totally consumed.

_____ As the *hametz* burns, recite the *Bi'ur hametz* formula in Aramaic and English.

_____ Take the *hametz* collected in the search the night before, plus any leftover *hametz* from the morning's breakfast, and place it in an empty coffee can or similar container or in an outdoor barbecue.

_____ Douse the *hametz* with lighter fluid or place some paper for fuel in the container with the *hametz*.

THE *HAMETZ* IN MY LIFE

The rabbis considered *hametz* symbolic of the *"yetzer ha-ra,"* the inclination to the negative in each of us. *Hametz* is that which bloats us, makes us arrogant, boastful, enslaving, unjust, revengeful.

List five things which are *"hametz"* in your life.

1. _____

_____

2. _____

_____

3. _____

_____

4. _____

_____

5. _____

_____

KOSHER FOR *PESAH* COUNTDOWN

T iming your preparations for Passover is critically important. Next to each step, indicate when you plan to complete the task listed:

TASK	TARGET DATE
Clean cupboards	_____
Clean the household	_____
Kasher the sink	_____
Pesah shopping	_____
Store *Pesah* supplies	_____
Kasher the stove	_____
Kasher pots and utensils	_____
Kasher the refrigerator	_____
Prepare Seder foods	_____
Bedikat hametz	_____
Bi'ur Hametz	_____
Mekhirat Hametz	_____
Cook	_____

PESAH 301: HAGGADAH FLUENCY

OBJECTIVES:

1. To be able to read with fluency major sections of the *Haggadah* in the original Hebrew or Aramaic.
2. To learn the meaning of these texts.
3. To learn how to chant these texts.

PESAH 301: FLUENCY CHART

As you learn to read, understand, and sing the following sections of the *Haggadah*, mark your progress on this chart:

TEXT	READ	UNDERSTAND	SING
ACT ONE			
CANDLE LIGHTING	____	____	____
KIDDUSH	____	____	____
KARPAS	____	____	____
HA LAHMA ANYA	____	____	____
ACT TWO			
MAH NISHTANAH	____	____	____
AVADIM HAYINU	____	____	____
BARUKH HA-MAKOM	____	____	____
ARBA'AH BANIM	____	____	____
METIHILA OVDEI	____	____	____
BARUKH SHOMER	____	____	____
V'HI SHE'AMDAH	____	____	____
TZEI U-L'MAD	____	____	____
ARAMI OVED AVI	____	____	____
ESER MAKOT	____	____	____
DAYYENU	____	____	____
RABBAN GAMLIEL	____	____	____
B'KHOL DOR VA-DOR	____	____	____
L'FIKHAKH	____	____	____
V'NOMAR L'FANAV	____	____	____
GA'AL YISRAEL	____	____	____
KOS SHEINI	____	____	____

ACT THREE

ROHTZAH   _____   _____   _____

MOTZI/MATZAH   _____   _____   _____

MAROR   _____   _____   _____

KOREKH   _____   _____   _____

BAREKH   _____   _____   _____

KOS SH'LISHI   _____   _____   _____

ACT FOUR

SHFOKH HAMATEKHA   _____   _____   _____

ELIYAHU HA-NAVI   _____   _____   _____

HALLEL   _____   _____   _____

Z'MIROT   _____   _____   _____

SEFIRAT HA-OMER   _____   _____   _____

KOS R'VI'I   _____   _____   _____

NIRTZAH   _____   _____   _____

PESAḤ 401: PESAḤ SEDER LEADING

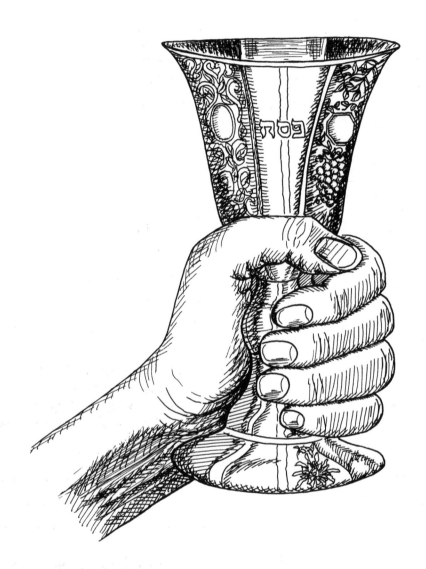

OBJECTIVES:

1. To learn how to study the *midrashic* sections of the *Haggadah*.
2. To learn how to "make *Midrash*" at your Seder.
3. To learn creative ideas for Seder leading.

READING *MIDRASH*

Midrash is a Jewish art form. It starts as a way of reading and responding to the biblical text. It becomes a way of thinking. The *Haggadah*, the road map to the Passover Seder, is a *midrashic* work; it weaves together an original vision of the story of the Exodus, spun from *midrashic* readings of biblical sources. Understanding how *midrash* works helps us understand the story being told.

Let's start with a biblical text. This is Exodus 6:6-8. God is talking with Moses, right after Moses' first encounter with Pharaoh and just before beginning the cycle of the plagues:

Therefore, say to the Children of Israel:
"I am the Lord.
I will bring you out from beneath the burdens of Egypt.
I will rescue you from your slavery to them.
I will redeem you with an outstretched arm and with great acts of judgment.
I will take you to Me as a people and I will be for you as a God.
And you will know that I am the Lord Your God
who brings you out from beneath the burdens of Egypt.
I will bring you into the land over which I lifted My hand
and promised to give it to Abraham, to Isaac, and to Jacob.
I will give it to you as a possession."

The rabbis read Torah with a number of assumptions. The most important of these was the belief that God authored the entire Torah. As a Divine document, it is supposed to be perfect--the world's best written communication. One of the implications of this assumption about authorship is that nothing in the text should be repeated without a purpose. God would say nothing extra (and would not waste time emphasizing). Rather, every repetition should be a clue to an extra level of meaning.

Where are the repetitions in this biblical selection? _____

_____

_____

Here is a selection from *Exodus Rabbah* (6:4)—a book of the *Midrash*. Look at the way the rabbis deal with this repetition.

There are here four expressions of redemption:
I will bring you out, I will rescue you, I will redeem you, and I will take you.
Each of these matches one of the four evil decrees which Pharaoh made about them:

There rose a new King over Egypt who knew not Joseph. He said to his people:
"Here, the nation of the Children of Israel are many and stronger than we.
Let's outsmart them." (Ex. 1:10)

The King of Egypt spoke to the Hebrew's midwives...
"When you help the Hebrew women deliver a baby and you see that it is a boy, kill it.
If it is a girl, she may live." (Ex. 1:15-16)

Pharaoh commanded his whole people:
Every Hebrew son which is born you will throw in the river. The daughters can live. (Ex. 1:22)

So, that day Pharaoh commanded the slave-drivers...
You are no longer to give straw to the people to make the bricks...(Ex. 5:6-7)

(By the way, these are the only four times that Pharaoh gives orders regarding the Jewish people.)

The rabbis established that the four cups which are drunk on the eve of Passover
are to stand for these four expressions. It is a way to fulfill the verse:
I will lift up the cup of redemption, and call upon the name of the Lord. (Ps. 116:13)

Let's analyze the *midrash*.

1. What is the problem this *midrash* was written to solve?

_____

_____

2. How does it solve this problem?

_____

_____

3. What central idea does this *midrash* introduce?

_____

_____

4. What message(s) does this *midrash* teach?

_____

_____

The *Haggadah* uses this same *midrashic* pattern in many places. One classic example is near the end of the *Maggid* section where four biblical verses tell the story of the Exodus. Read these verses and mark the repetitions:

And he (Jacob) went down to Egypt and dwelt there few in number and there became a nation: great, mighty, and numerous.

The Egyptians ill-treated us, oppressed us, and made us do slave-labor.

We cried to the Lord, the God of our ancestors
And the Lord heard our voice--God saw our ill-treatment
our burden and our oppression.

The Lord brought us out of Egypt with a strong hand, an outstretched arm,
with great fear, with signs, and wonders.

Deut. 26:5-8

Now look in the *Maggid* section of your *Haggadah*. Find the answers given by the rabbis. Examine the messages they built around these repetitions.

ORIGINAL *MIDRASHIM*

In *Building Jewish Life: Passover* (a book written by Joel Lurie Grishaver and published by *Torah Aura Productions*), six children tell their own story of the Exodus from Egypt. Here are some of their original *midrashim*:

My name is Judi with a i and a circle over it and I am twelve. When I was a slave, I used to dream a lot. My mother used to put me to bed at night with stories of the land that God had promised to our father Abraham. I used to dream that those promises came true.

Kent—Age 9. When I was a slave in Egypt, I worked as a boy in the stone quarries. I spent all day carrying a heavy jug of water from work team to work team. It was hard work--and that jar was heavy. But I felt good about my job--because the water I carried helped to keep other Jews alive.

Gabe and I'm seven and three-quarters. When I was just born, my mother hid me at the bottom of the laundry basket. When I was two, they hid seven of us boys in a cave, and my sister took care of us. When I turned three, they brought me home--but they made me wear a stupid dress. I hated that. By the time I was five, they just let me go to work in the fields and the hiding ended. THANK GOD!

Your family, too, can engage in performing one of Passover's prime *mitzvot* by telling a personal version of the story of how you left Egypt. You can create that original string of *midrashim* by answering six questions. (Meanwhile, as leader, you can practice your answers below.)

1. What was it like to be a slave? What job did you have?

_____

_____

2. What did you hate about being a slave? Did you like anything?

_____

_____

3. When Moses said that you would soon be free, what did you think about?

_____

_____

4. What was it like during the plagues?

_____

_____

5. When you left Egypt, what did you take with you?

_____

_____

6. What is the best part about being free?

_____

_____

CREATIVE SEDER LEADING

In class, you will spend time brainstorming some wonderful ideas for leading a creative Seder. In preparation for that discussion, write down two ideas of your own (or two of the ideas you liked best in the textbook).

_____

_____

_____

_____

_____

_____

_____

_____

_____

During your class discussion, write down four or five of the best suggestions that are shared.

_____

_____

_____

_____

_____

_____

_____

_____

_____

_____

_____

_____

_____

_____

_____

_____

_____

_____

_____

PESAH 501:
INVOLVING CHILDREN
IN THE PASSOVER EXPERIENCE

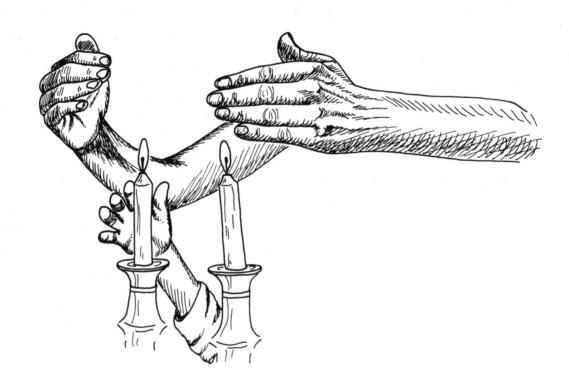

OBJECTIVES:

1. To categorize portions of the Seder which are designed to captivate children.
2. To develop plans for involving children in the Seder celebration in a meaningful way.

YOUR CHILDHOOD MEMORIES OF SEDER

On this page, write in several of the strongest memories you have of Seder as a child. (If you have no childhood memories of Seder, think of memories of any holiday celebration in the home.)

WHEN I THINK OF SEDER AS A CHILD, I REMEMBER...

_____

_____

_____

_____

_____

_____

MEMORIES I WANT TO CREATE FOR CHILDREN AT MY SEDER ARE...

_____

_____

_____

_____

_____

Activity Two: Planning for Children
Purpose: *To select those Seder moments which will be used to focus on children.*

SEDER MEMORIES I WANT TO GIVE MY CHILDREN/GRANDCHILDREN

Put a K in front of each step which you believe will "automatically" interest or involve children.
Put a D in front of each step which you believe will be difficult for children.
Circle two or three of the D steps which you would most like to transform to a K.
Brainstorm activities which could enable this transformation.

ACT ONE: The Beginning

_____ Prologue: Candle Lighting   _____

_____ Kadesh, Urhatz Mnemonic   _____

_____ Kadesh (Kiddush)   _____

_____ Urhatz   _____

_____ Karpas   _____

_____ Yahatz   _____

_____ Ha Lahma Anya   _____

ACT TWO: *MAGGID*—The Tellings

_____ Mah Nishtanah   _____

_____ Avadim Hayinu   _____

_____ Barukh ha-Makom   _____

_____ Arba'ah Banim   _____

_____ Metihila Ovdei Avodah Zarah   _____

_____ Barukh Shomer/ V'hi She'amdah   _____

_____ Tzei u'L-mad   _____

_____ Arami Oved Avi   _____

_____ Eser Makot   _____

_____ Dayyenu   _____

_____ Rabban Gamliel Hayah Omer   _____

_____ B'khol Dor va-Dor   _____

_____ L'fikhakh   _____

_____ V'nomar L'fanav   _____

_____ Ga'al Yisrael   _____

_____ Kos Sheini   _____

ACT THREE: The Feast

_____ Rohtzah

_____ Motzi/Matzah

_____ Maror

_____ Korekh

_____ Shulhan Orekh

_____ Tzafun

_____ Barekh

_____ Kos Sh'lishi

ACT FOUR: Redemption

_____ Shfokh Hamatekha

_____ Eliyahu ha-Navi

_____ Hallel

_____ Z'mirot

_____ Sefirat ha-Omer

_____ Kos R'vi'i

_____ Nirtzah

Now, write in 4-6 of the best steps before and during the Seder ceremony for children to be involved. Then, write some notes to yourself about what the children can do:

BEFORE THE SEDER:

1._____

2._____

3._____

DURING THE SEDER:

1._____

2._____

3._____

4._____

5._____

6._____

NOTES: _____

_____

_____

PESAH 601:
CREATIVE PASSOVER COOKERY

OBJECTIVES

1. To identify your favorite Passover foods.
2. To share creative Passover recipes.

MY FAVORITE PASSOVER FOODS

Here is a list of classic Passover foods. Mark your favorites and indicate which you plan to make this year.

_____   Gefilte fish

_____   *Matzah* brei

_____   *Haroset*

_____   *Tzimmes*

_____   Chopped liver

_____   *Gribines*

_____   Mandel cookies

_____   *Taiglach*

_____   Chicken soup

_____   *Matzah* balls (*Kneidlach*)

_____   Brisket

_____   Chicken

_____   Asparagus

_____   Rhubarb

_____   *Meyina*

_____   Hard-boiled eggs

_____   Desserts

_____

_____

_____

_____

GREAT *PESAH* RECIPES

In the spaces below, fill in favorite *Pesah* recipes shared in class.

_____

_____
_____
_____
_____
_____

_____

_____
_____
_____
_____
_____

_____

_____
_____
_____
_____

_____

_____
_____
_____
_____
_____

APPENDIX—CREATIVE *PESAH* IDEAS

We are proud to present a number of creative *Pesah* craft and celebration ideas that you can use to enhance your Seder. Most of the ideas originally appeared in *Chicken Soup: A Magazine to Nourish Jewish Family Life*, edited by Judy Bin-Nun, Susie Wolfson, and Ron Wolfson, published by the Clejan Educational Resources Center of the University of Judaism.

The Art of Jewish Living: The Passover Seder textbook lists many creative ideas for Seder celebration. Use this checklist of innovative ideas as you organize your Seder celebration. The page number refers to the place in the textbook where the idea is explained.

—Light one *yom tov* candle for each member of the family (p. 69).

—Chant *Kadesh, Urhatz* before each step of the Seder (p. 74).

—Prepare a *Kadesh, Urhatz* poster or table cards (p. 74).

—Provide *Karpas* appetizers (p. 99).

—Reenact the Exodus, Sephardic style, at *Yahatz* (p. 105) or *Avadim Hayinu* (p. 130).

—Break the middle *matzah* into the shape of a *dalet* and vav or a *hei* (p. 105).

—Pass the Seder plate over each person's head during *Ha Lahma Anya* (p. 113).

—Distribute nuts to the children at *Mah Nishtanah* (p. 125).

—Ask a set of modern "4 Questions" (p. 125).

—Have an *Avadim Hayinu* skit (p. 130).

—Prepare a chart with the four verses of Deuteronomy 26:5-8 for following during the *Maggid* (p. 151).

—Integrate songs and stories that tell the Exodus story (p. 151).

—List Ten Plagues that "plague" us today (p. 156).

—"Beat" each other with scallions during *Dayyenu* (p. 159).

—Use a creative *afikomen* hunt idea (see this Workbook) (p. 199).

—Save part of the *afikomen* from year to year (p. 199).

—Pass Elijah's cup for everyone to contribute to it (p. 212).

—Set an extra place for Elijah (p. 213 and 215).

—Dedicate a Fifth Cup of Wine for Israel (p. 214).

—Dedicate a *Matzah* of Hope (p. 214).

—Take an Elijah walk (p. 215).

—Create an *Omer* counting chart (p. 227)

—Sing *Hatikvah* at the conclusion of the Seder (p. 231).

—Add supplementary readings throughout the ceremony (p. 254).

—Invite guests to prepare commentaries (pp. 257 ff).

—Make your own *Midrash* (p. 259).

—Plan children's activities at the Seder (pp. 260 ff).

—Create *Tzedakah* opportunities around the Passover holiday (pp. 263 ff).

—Write a parody of a Seder song (p. 265).

—Acquire *Matzah Shmurah* for the Seder (p. 274).

—Have a *hametz* party before Passover (p. 280).

—Plan a creative *Bedikat Hametz* ceremony (p. 299).

—Save your lulav to use during the Search for Leaven and the Burning of Leven (pp. 299 and 304).

—Prepare individualized Seder plates (p. 316).

—Host a *Maimuna*, (end of Passover celebration) (p. 322).

AFIKOMEN JUMBLE WORD SEARCH

Searching for the *afikomen* can be one of the most exciting moments of your *Pesah* Seder, especially for the children. However, sometimes the search ends in unhappy kids who, year after year, search in vain for the prized piece of *matzah*.

Here's an idea for the *afikomen* search that allows every child to "find" something that will uncover the elusive hiding place. In that sense, it includes everyone in the search, even the adults!

1. Prepare a chart with the *Kadesh, Urhatz* mnemonic listed as:

KADESH	A	MAROR	O
URHATZ	R	KOREKH	E
KARPAS	R	SHULHAN OREKH	R
YAHATZ	T	TZAFUN	F
MAGGID	G	BAREKH	R
ROHTZAH	T	HALLEL	E
MOTZI/MATZAH	I	NIRTZAH	A

(Use the chart during the Seder to alert your guests where you are in the course of the ceremony. They may ask about the underlined letters. Tell them they'll find out at *afikomen* time.)

2. Notice one letter is underlined in each word. Write each letter on a single 3x5 index card.

3. When it's time to hide the *afikomen*, or before your guests arrive for Seder, hide each of the 14 cards around the house.

4. At *Tzafun*, the *afikomen* must be found and redeemed. Before the children are sent to look for it, tell them that this year, you have a new way to find the *afikomen*. Show them an example of the index card. Tell them that 14 cards have been hidden throughout the house. All 14 must be found to solve the word jumble which is the clue to where the *afikomen* is hidden. Set a limit as to how many cards one child can find; i.e., if you have 7 children, each child can find two cards—after that, they must stop searching. (This allows all the children to find cards.)

5. When all the cards have been found, ask the adults at the table to try to solve the two-word "word jumble" that will reveal the clue to where the *afikomen* is. The answer to the jumble is on the bottom of this page. When the clue is solved, all the children can run to the place where the *afikomen* can be found (be sure the leader hides it there!) and they all have found the *afikomen*. All the children should then receive an *afikomen* prize.

6. You can create your own different clues by choosing different letters from each of the 14 words.

Answer: AT REFRIGERATOR

FREEDOM PLATES

Here's a wonderful idea to personalize one of the major Passover themes.

Before the first Seder, provide your family and/or guests with 9 inch paper plates that have a pre-drawn Star of David in the center. Write each person's name in the center of the star. Have old magazines, glue and scissors on hand. Ask each participant to find magazine pictures according to the following plan:

1. Find three pictures of things that make you feel free.

2. Find three pictures of things that make you feel like a slave. (Younger children can pick six "feeling free" pictures.)

3. Paste the cut-out pictures at the points of the star--freedom on the left side and slavery on the right.

4. Share the plates during the *Maggid* section of your Seder.

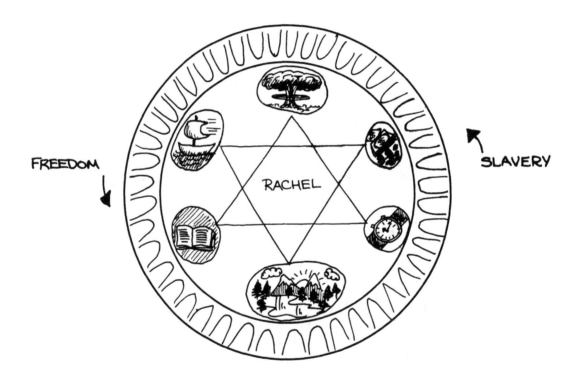

FREEDOM

SLAVERY

RACHEL

LABELS' KOSHER FOR *PESAH* TABLE MAT

This is an ecologically sound and clever keepsake for *Pesahdik* family meals. You'll need:

  12x18 inch construction paper in your choice of color
  scissors
  white glue
  clear contact paper
  a collection of *Pesah* food item labels, such as the logo from a box of *matzah*, jelly, macaroons, wine, etc.

Here's how:

1. Cut out the labels and arrange in a pleasing fashion on the construction paper mat. Be sure the entire surface is covered.

2. Glue the labels in place and allow to dry.

3. Cover the front and back of the mat with clear contact paper.

4. Use at *Pesah* meal times.

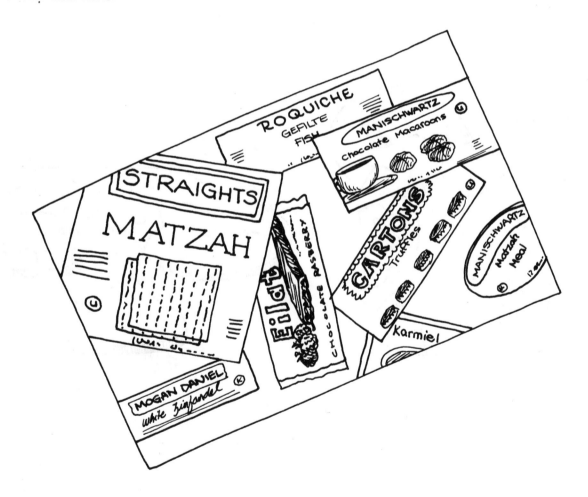

BEDIKAT ḤAMETZ SEARCH

The *Bedikat Hametz* search the night before Passover is one of the best family activities of the year. One variation we've tried is this:

1. Take a piece of construction paper and draw a picture of a bread slice.

2. Create ten segments on the paper.

3. Cut out the ten pieces. If you wish, you can glue real bread crumbs (or Fritos or Cheerios) to each piece.

4. Hide the ten pieces of the bread slice puzzle in different parts of the house.

5. Conduct the *Bedikat Hametz* search as described in the textbook.

6. At the conclusion of the search, piece together the bread slice puzzle.

7. Now, store the *"ḥametz"* for *Bi'ur Ḥametz* the next morning.

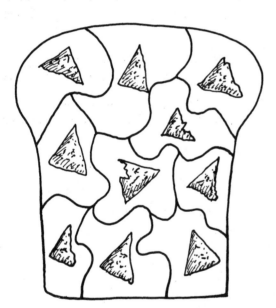
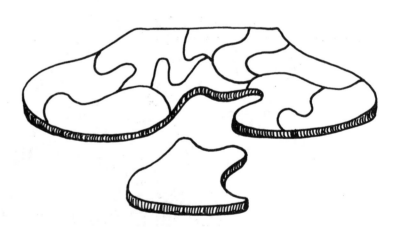

PESAḤ APPETIZERS

Here's a wonderfully creative Passover appetizer idea for your guests to enjoy while gathering for the Seder.

The centerpiece of your appetizer tray is an avocado "froggy," surrounded by "bullrush babes 'n baskets."

YOU'LL NEED:

  1 large ripe avocado
  2 large red radishes
  Toothpicks
  Plastic "google" eyes (or construction paper cut-out eyes)
  1 dozen small eggs
  1 jar of gefilte fishlets (drained)
  Horseradish
  Parsley
  Raw vegetables

HERE'S HOW:

Cut out a "V"-shaped slice from the larger end of the avocado to form the frog's mouth. Cut one radish in half to form eyes, slice a radish stick for the red tongue and attach with toothpicks to the avocado base. Use a dab of water to "glue" the google eyes to bring out the frog's personality! Place the frog in a parsley-filled dish in the center of a large tray.

To make the "babes 'n baskets," hardboil a dozen small eggs. Cool, then slice them in half, removing the yolk. Your egg whites form the basket which you fill with one gefilte fishlet, each dabbed with horseradish.

Now, cut up raw vegetables—green peppers, radishes, carrots, celery, cucumbers, cherry tomatoes, and mushrooms—and mound in a pleasing arrangement around the "froggy" and the "bullrush babes 'n baskets."

PERSONAL SEDER PLATES

Here is a wonderful way to provide each of your Seder guests with an individual Seder plate.

For each personal Seder plate you plan to make, YOU'LL NEED:

    1 large shelled hard boiled egg
    1 radish with its stringy end (not the green end) still intact
    2 cloves
    2 slices of green pepper
    1 slice of red pepper
    Toothpicks
    Bed of parsley
    3 gefilte fish balls
    Horseradish

HERE'S HOW:

The objective is to create a "bird" out of the required Seder plate objects. The shelled egg forms the body of the bird. Firmly press two cloves into the radish; these become the eyes. Attach the radish to the wider end of the egg using a toothpick; the point of the radish becomes the beak of the bird. Poke a toothpick through the center of the egg and place slices of green pepper on both sides to form the wings of the bird. Put one toothpick in the back of the egg and attach a piece of red pepper to form the tail. Place the entire bird on a bed of parsley. Add three gefilte fish balls and a dab of horseradish for decoration. If you like, you can also add a sliver of horseradish root.

PESAH PILLOW PLACECARD

Create puffy placecards for those inclined to recline. This is a cooperative family craft and a special souvenir for your Seder guests.

You'll need (per guest):
  2 9x12 sheets of felt
  Tacky (craft) glue
  Extra sheets of felt for decorative designing
  Sharpie thin point permanent markers in assorted colors
  Optional—rick-rack, seam binding, sequins and the like
  Batting to use for stuffing.

Here's the scoop to form one pillow placecard. Glue together 3 sides of the 2 felt sheets to form a pillow case. When completely dry, stuff case with batting and then close the remaining side with glue. You now have a mini-pillow ready for surface decoration. Be sure to write with permanent marker each guest and/or family member's name on their pillow. This is the placecard portion. Add Spring or *Pesah* theme felt cut-outs by gluing them directly onto the pillow. Felt cut-outs can include—Kiddush cup, *matzah,* an only kid, Pyramids & palm trees, baby in basket, bull rushes, frogs, parsley, flowers, shankbone, bricks & mortar, egg, Moses with staff, Red Sea and more—use your "*Pesah* imagination!!" Rick-rack, sequins and the like can be added visuals for zippy embellishment. Place each pillow, name side up, on your dining room chairs and you're ready to answer the Four Questions with style!

THE BALLAD OF THE FOUR SONS

A very popular parody of the Four Children (Four Sons) was written by Ben Aronin. Families with young children seem to especially enjoy including this when the Four Children are discussed:

(To the tune "My Darlin' Clementine")

Said the father to his children:
"At the Seder you will dine
You will eat your fill of *matzah*
You will drink four cups of wine."

Now this father had no daughters
But his sons they numbered four:
One was wise and one was wicked;
One was simple and a bore.

And the fourth was sweet and winsome
He was young and he was small.
While his brothers asked the questions
He could barely speak at all.

Said the wise son to his father
"Could you please explain the laws
of the customs of the Seder?
Could you please explain the cause?"

And the father proudly answered:
"Every man himself must see
In every age and generation
As if he himself were freed."

Then the wicked son said wickedly:
"What does all this mean to *you?*"
And the father's voice was bitter
As his grief and anger grew.

"If yourself you don't consider
As a son of *Yisrael,*
Then for you this has no meaning;
You could be a slave as well."

Then the simple son said simply:
"What is this?" and quietly
The good father told his offspring
"We were freed from slavery."

And the youngest was silent
For he was not very bold.
But his eyes grew wide with wonder
As the *Pesah* tale was told.

Now dear children, heed the lesson
And remember ever more
The good father and his children
And his sons that numbered four.

Ben Aronin

Notes

Notes